EXPLORING
BUSINESS
AND
ECONOMICS

EXPLORING
BUSINESS
AND
ECONOMICS

Money
and
Banking

Norman L. Macht

Chelsea House Publishers
Philadelphia

Frontis: Governments are free to print as much or as little of their money as they want in circulation. What the money is worth depends on what you can buy with it.

CHELSEA HOUSE PUBLISHERS

EDITOR-IN-CHIEF Sally Cheney
DIRECTOR OF PRODUCTION Kim Shinners
PRODUCTION MANAGER Pamela Loos
ART DIRECTOR Sara Davis

Choptank Syndicate/Chestnut Productions

EDITORIAL Norman Macht and Mary Hull
PRODUCTION Lisa Hochstein
PICTURE RESEARCH Norman Macht

http://www.chelseahouse.com

First Printing

1 3 5 7 9 8 6 4 2

Library of Congress Cataloging-in-Publication Data

Macht, Norman L. (Norman Lee), 1929–
    Money and banking / Norman Macht
    p. cm. – (Exploring business and economics)
    ISBN 0-7910-6636-3 (alk. paper)
1. Money. 2. Banks and banking. I. Title. II. Series.
HG221.M1244 2001
332.1—dc21   2001042511

Table of Contents

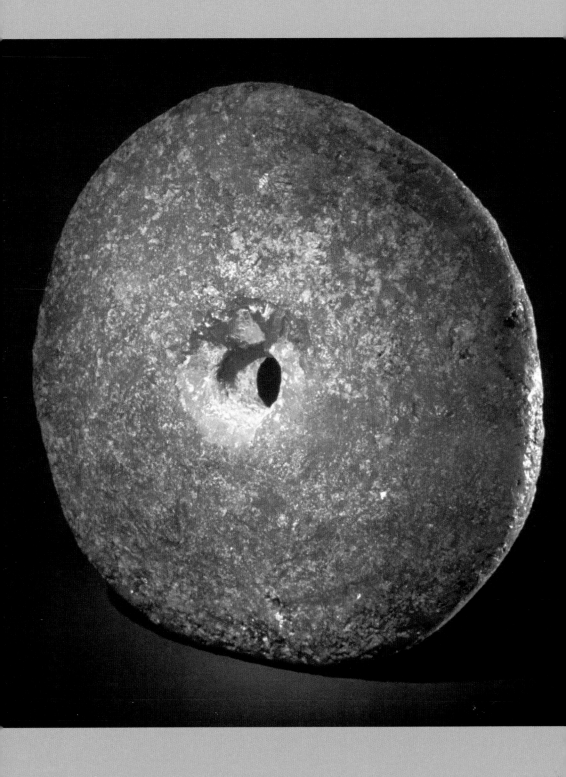

Limestone found on an island 400 miles away is used to carve the large and pocket-size coins used as money on the South Pacific island of Yap. This 12-foot high coin, called a rai, might represent the entire wealth of a Yap family.

What Is Money

The American author Mark Twain once wrote, "Some men worship rank, some worship heroes, some worship power, some worship God, and over these ideals they dispute—but they all worship money."

Except for health—and sometimes even at the cost of their health—**money** is the most important thing in some people's lives. Even people who already have more money than they can ever spend may devote their lives to making more of it. Ask people why they hold the jobs they have, or do the kind of work they do, and the answer is often "for the money," not for the love of the work they're doing to earn it.

Writers and philosophers have long been fascinated by people's attitudes toward money. "The love of money is the root of all evil," is an oft-quoted adage from the Bible. Two thousand years ago a Roman poet, Juvenal, wrote:

"Some men make money not for the sake of living but ache in the blindness of greed and live just for their fortune's sake."

It is easier to earn money than it is to manage it wisely once you have it. One of the most sensitive nerves in the human body is the one that goes to the pocketbook or

Money Isn't Everything

According to a Greek myth, there was once a king named Midas. Midas liked money, which in those days meant gold. It was important to him to have more gold than anyone else.

One day Midas did a favor for a friend of one of the gods. The god rewarded Midas by giving him the gift that would please Midas the most. The god told Midas, "From now on, everything you touch will turn to gold."

Midas was the happiest person in the kingdom. Whatever he touched—dirt, rocks, weeds—instantly turned to gold. Soon he had more gold than anyone in the world. But there was a problem. Because everything he touched turned to gold, which included things like bread and meat and fruit, Midas couldn't eat anything. He was the richest of kings, but he was also the unhappiest.

Midas appealed to the god to take away his power. The god told him he must bathe in a certain river to wash away his golden touch. Midas did as he was told and the sand in the river bottom was the last thing he touched that became gold. Today, when someone has the ability to make money in any kind of business they go into, that person is said to have "the Midas touch."

E 1030085

Many immigrants arrived in America with their pockets full of money like these Polish zlotys, only to find that the money was worthless because nobody in America would accept it.

wallet! Among American families, money is the most common source of arguments. A husband may think his wife spends too much on things for herself; a wife may become upset when the husband buys something expensive for himself. They both may yell at the kids for pestering them for money, or saying, "buy me this," or "can I have that?" or "the other kids have one," too often. The tension increases when they get over their heads with bills and credit card debts.

Then there are people who don't like to spend any of their money, no matter how much they have. Once in a while stories appear in newspapers about people who lived as though they were too poor to buy food or have electric lights, and when they died their relatives discovered that they had hoarded thousands—even millions—of dollars, hidden under floorboards or in boxes in the attic.

These people are called misers. A miser is someone who lives as if they have no money at all, when they really have lots of money hidden away. A woman named Hetty Green was like that. She lived in New York in the early 1900s and was the richest woman in the world. But she lived in a tiny furnished apartment, ate crackers for lunch because she wouldn't spend the money to go into a restaurant, and refused to take her children to a doctor when they had health problems because it cost too much.

Wealth gives people the means to buy anything they want. It also gives them a standing in the community, influence, and respect. The rich are considered smarter and somehow better than the average person, even if they aren't.

"With money in your pocket, you are wise and you are handsome and you sing well too," says a Yiddish proverb.

Your attitude toward money and its importance in your life may be shaped by what you see and hear around you while you are growing up. But similar experiences and environments don't always produce the same results in people.

Camel Dung Wealth

During World War II there were people living in Siberia, where it was so cold the temperature could go down to 90 degrees below zero. For six months of the year everything was frozen solid. The only way to get any water was to melt the ice and snow. The only way to do that—and to keep warm—was to build a fire. But there was no wood, coal, or oil. There was only one source of fuel: frozen camel dung. Possessing some camel dung meant the difference between life and death. It was worth more than money. You could have saddlebags full of money and nobody would sell you their precious camel dung. Desperate men with pockets full of money died trying to steal it.

This Roman 22-carat gold coin was discovered in London during work for a construction project. The coin dates from the era of Roman rule in Britain and may have been minted as early as 54 A.D. The Romans were among the first to decorate their coins with the heads of emperors and gods.

During the **Great Depression** of the 1930s, millions of American workers were unemployed. They had no money to provide for their families. Many were unable to make the **mortgage** payments on their homes or farms, and became homeless. Others lost whatever money they had saved when the **banks** closed.

These experiences left deep emotional scars. Young people who grew up during those years of poverty reacted in different ways. Some refused to buy anything on credit or by borrowing money for a house or car. They were afraid they might lose it if it wasn't fully paid for, so they paid cash for everything and never took out loans. Others, remembering a childhood with no toys, no new clothes, sometimes nothing to eat, grew up determined to buy and enjoy everything in life, whether or not they could afford it. They ran up credit card balances and other debts without a care, digging financial holes from which they could never climb out. Their motto seemed to be, "buy everything you want, never pay for it, and die owing everybody."

"Almost any man knows how to earn money," wrote American philosopher Henry Thoreau, "but not one in a million knows how to spend it."

Recognizing that a single economic zone was more efficient than 11 different ones, in 2002 the European Union countries began replacing their individual currencies with a new unit of currency known as the euro, shown above.

The people who are most contented when it comes to money are those who know how to earn it, how to spend it, and how to save it. They have achieved a healthy, balanced, objective attitude toward it. They see money for what it is: a useful tool and not an end in itself.

For what, after all, is money? Hold a one dollar bill in your hand and look at it. What do you see? A small rectangle of a special kind of paper covered with words, numbers, and pictures in black and green ink. Put different words, number, and pictures on it, and it becomes a 5 or 10 or 100 or 1,000 dollar bill. They will buy more than a one dollar bill, but they're still just paper and ink.

What good is money? You can't eat it, wear it, use it to keep the rain off your head, or keep you warm. The fact is money has no intrinsic value. A piece of money is worthless by itself. It gets its value only from whatever you can exchange it for, and that value is constantly changing.

A dollar bill may equal a hamburger at a fast food place, but not at a ballpark or a fancy restaurant. If the price of a gallon of gasoline goes from $1 to $2, your dollar bill will buy only half as much as it did before. Your money has lost half its worth in gasoline. This shrinking of the value of money is called **inflation.** We'll explain that more in Chapter Five.

The value of your money can depend on where you are. For money to have any value, it must be acceptable to the person you're trying to give it to. Other countries issue their own money, but it may be worthless outside of that country. A Canadian dollar can be spent in any Canadian store, but if you try to use it to pay for something in an American store, the merchant may not accept it. And he doesn't have to. If you need something in a hurry and foreign money is all you have, it may be worthless because of where you happen to be standing at the time. You're no better off than someone with empty pockets.

During the great wave of emigration from Europe between 1890 and 1920, some emigrants who had been wealthy in the old country arrived in America with trunks full of Russian or Polish or other Eastern European currencies. When they landed, they discovered the money was worthless in America. They couldn't spend it because nobody would take it. They couldn't exchange it because there weren't any exchange bureaus for those types of **currency.** Suddenly they were paupers. The only thing the money was good for was to start a fire.

Everyone in the United States is required to accept currency (money) issued by the U.S. government to pay for goods or settle debts. That's why it's called legal tender: money tendered or offered as payment that must be accepted by the seller.

The first American paper currency was called the "Continental." At times the paper dollar was so devalued that the saying "not worth a Continental" was coined. Printed in Philadelphia, Pennsylvania, every bill—as many as 4,800 a day—had to be signed by hand.

The same is true of coins. An American coin is a piece of metal alloy—copper and nickel. Coins are minted for convenience, to make it easier to buy and sell things without the need to price everything in exact dollars. Without coins there would be no 75-cent candy bars or 50-cent sodas.

Money doesn't have to be made of paper or metal. It can be—and has been—sheep, stones, shark teeth, beads, shells, human beings, tea, salt, feathers—whatever the people in a community agree to accept in exchange for goods and labor.

Today we are accustomed to going into a store or gas station or restaurant and buying what we want or need. It's hard to imagine life without money. But that's the way the world was for thousands of years. Even after the use of money became widespread, there were societies, including colonial America, where money was rarely seen or used.

People lived, even prospered, without money. How do you think they did it?

Much of the business done in general stores in the old West like this one in Pie Town, New Mexico, was by bartering. Farmers and ranchers didn't have much cash. They would bring a calf or some corn or chickens to the store and swap it for flour and sugar and other basic supplies.

Barter and Trade

Imagine that you are sitting in the school cafeteria at lunch time. Your mother has packed a peanut butter sandwich for your lunch. But you're tired of peanut butter. You notice the person sitting next to you has a baloney sandwich.

"Want to swap sandwiches?" you ask.

"Okay," the other person says.

And you swap. There was no money involved. Even if there were no such thing as money, you could still trade what you had for something you wanted.

That's the way people lived for thousands of years—by **barter,** exchanging something they didn't need or want for something they wanted or needed more. The Masai tribe in Africa raised livestock but grew no crops. They lived on the meat and milk from their animals. Other tribes were farmers, who raised more crops than they needed. The Masai could swap their animals to these farmers in exchange for grain and vegetables. In this way, each group provided the other with what they needed.

Societies throughout Asia and the Middle East existed in the same way. If one group was good at making tools or clay pots, they could trade these items for the food they needed. If no neighboring groups had any camels or animal skins to trade, they had to survive without those things.

During the Middle Ages, a period of time from about A.D. 500 to 1500, most people in Europe never saw any money. Workers known as **serfs** were dependent on the land, and the owners of the land, for their survival. What little trade that took place was by bartering.

Barter often involved bargaining. There were no fixed rates of exchange, such as "one cow equals 50 potatoes." The two trading parties had to agree on the terms of the deal.

In order to strike a bargain, both sides in the deal must be satisfied with the outcome. For example, suppose you want

Trade Brings Columbus to the Americas

Christopher Columbus's first voyage in 1492 was intended to find what he thought would be a shorter route to Japan, China, and the islands of the South Pacific. He hoped to gain a competitive edge over other trading nations. Queen Isabella of Spain financed the voyage because Columbus promised to bring back great wealth. At the first islands he came to, he bartered brass bells and glass beads for food and gold.

For thousands of years, European traders did business by loading caravans with goods and traveling throughout Africa and Asia. They would exchange their goods for things the Europeans wanted, such as silks and spices, which could be found only in faraway places.

a Cal Ripken Jr. rookie baseball card and your friend has two of them. You might say, "I'll trade you two Mickey Mantle cards for a Ripken rookie."

"No way," he says. "I want three Mantle cards."

"How about two Mantles and a Sammy Sosa?" you say.

If he accepts your offer, it's a deal. But it took a lot of negotiating to close it.

Now why would your friend want two Mickey Mantle cards? He may already have one. Perhaps he now has what he needs to trade with somebody else for a Mark McGwire.

Throughout history, all kinds of things have been useful or valuable as items to be bartered. Called **commodities,** these items ranged from nails to salt to human beings.

People could be bartered as slaves or voluntary workers. A man might barter his labor in exchange for passage to a foreign land. A father might allow a man to marry his daughter in exchange for two blankets and a goat. Muslim traders in North Africa bartered guns, fabric, and horses to tribal chiefs in exchange for slaves, ivory, and gold.

Bargaining was not always done face to face. In parts of Africa, Asia, and the islands of the South Pacific, silent bartering was the custom. Arriving on a foreign shore, traders would unload their cargo and leave it on the beach. The local clan would bring their trading goods and leave them. Since they had no common language, each side might add something to its pile until both sides considered it a fair exchange. In some remote areas, this kind of trading took place without the two sides ever seeing each other.

When people began to travel by foot or camel or boat, they discovered other parts of the world that had things they had never seen: gold, copper, tea, salt, sugar, spices, ivory, different kinds of wood, iron and bronze tools, and domestic animals like goats, cows, sheep, and horses. In turn, the travelers brought things that were new to the inhabitants of these distant lands. Everybody benefitted from these exchanges of goods, foods, and customs.

Barter became trade. What had been local swap meets became big business. As the demand for strange new foods and spices grew in Europe, the potential for large profits arose. Complications arose, too. How many horses was a shipload of slaves worth? How could you measure such things as gold, salt, pepper, tea, and nutmeg against guns, cloth, and beads? If a trader judged the quality of the dates or fish or slaves to be inferior, squabbles broke out over how many guns or horses they were worth. Sometimes the traveler had to take his ship or caravan still loaded with cargo to another place to try to make a deal. Traders tried to establish standards, but there were too many differences of opinion.

As trading activity increased, ships from the great trading ports of Venice, France, Holland, and England began venturing farther into the unknown. They sailed around Africa to China and westward to America. The business of trading became more organized. Trading posts were built. It was more efficient to collect a region's products from outlying areas and bring them to central stations on the coast where ships could anchor in the harbors.

Trade wars began between companies representing England, Holland, and Portugal. Each tried to gain control of sources of supply for exotic spices from the South Seas that were in large demand in Europe. Ships raced to bring their cargoes home first. Sometimes they attacked each other's ships and raided competitors' warehouses.

In the early 1500s, French traders and fur trappers began trading with the Indians of North America. The Indians had no use for French money so they bartered furs, buffalo skins, and blankets for weapons and tools that they could not make themselves.

Worth One's Salt

Roman soldiers were sometimes paid with salt (the origin of the word "salary"). Salt was more precious than gold. Used to cure and preserve meat at a time when there was no refrigeration, salt was more essential to life than gold. It was always in demand, and it was exchangeable for other goods. But it was risky; if the soldier spilled his salt, he could not easily pick it up.

Men have fought, died, endured years of bitter hardship, started wars, and searched the world for gold. At one time gold was believed to be the only reliable kind of wealth, and paper money was considered worthless unless it could be exchanged for gold. Some people still distrust paper money and keep some gold hidden in case of emergencies.

Bartering continued to be the principal means of doing business among the settlers of the American West even after it had been replaced by the use of money in eastern cities. There wasn't much cash on the western frontier. It was simpler to swap a crop of wheat or a newborn calf for food, shoes, a keg of nails, or a roll of barbed wire.

Peddlers pulling carts throughout the south and west operated on the same basis: pots and pans, mugs, thread, fabric, and pins and needles were exchanged for chickens, corn, butter, and eggs.

The barter system was based on one essential assumption: the person who had what you needed would be willing to take whatever you had to trade. If that wasn't the case, you did without whatever it was you needed. Although bartering continues to work in some parts of the world, it became evident as early as a few thousand years ago that, as societies grew, trade could not be wholly sustained without some more efficient means of payment.

Sueno Receuer dai camerai dai
presteri del Comui de Venecia co
mo apar per liquadermi del Comui.
Inpresteri senti Alorto conestier o
dco mathia de fremithi da muram
como Aparia qua de soto depostai
posta. Cum leconoriao In losestier de Santa ✠

Alprima Una posta · a dc de Lener · m · dz · ccc · xlvij · la
qual fese Scruer licomessarii de Gr piero bragadin i
legondo la forma del testamento del dito Gr piero · co
mo apar il amare de santa eraia de muri · lbr · cc · agsr

Item Una posta doi · m · de decenbrio · In · dz · ccc · xlviij · la
qual fese Scruer · Gr em de eura sento · per checho te

A 14th century illuminated manuscript from the Register of the Monastery of San Maffio in Venice depicts an early banking scene, with men counting coins and keeping records.

Early Money

Different societies found different ways to overcome the problems of bartering. It didn't matter what they used as a medium of exchange, as long as everybody agreed to accept it. It had to be something relatively scarce, but plentiful enough to cover the normal trading activity. It wouldn't work if whatever they used was too common or too rare.

Nobody would trade a goat for two rocks that they could pick up in a field themselves. And if there was only one lump of gold in the entire land, that wouldn't make much buying and selling possible. Whatever the group decided to use for money had to be uncommon enough to have some value in the eyes of the people. It was also essential that whatever they used could be counted or weighed. And, for convenience, the smaller, the better. Although the Egyptians used cattle and sheep for large-scale trading, this was hardly the kind of money a man could carry around in the marketplace.

For thousands of years, one of the most popular forms of money was the **cowrie shell,** especially the tiger cowrie. One of 150 kinds of cowries, the tiger is spotted like a leopard. These shiny round sea snails live in warm waters around China, India, Southeast Asia, the islands of the South Pacific, and Africa. Because they were accepted as money over a very wide area, cowries were very popular.

In China, tools such as hoes and knives were used as money. In the 10th century B.C., when they began to use copper and iron coins, the coins were shaped like miniature hoes and knives.

Beginning about 1600 A.D., Indians in the eastern part of North America used beads, called **wampum,** made from two kinds of shells: a sea snail called a whelk and a hard shell clam they called the quahog. Both were found in coastal salt waters from Canada to Florida. White beads were made from the whelks and purple ones from the quahog. The white beads were valued more highly than the purple, probably because they were scarcer or more difficult to create. The beads were tiny—eight of them measured one inch—and very difficult to make. The hard shells frequently broke. A hole was drilled in each bead so they could be strung together and made into necklaces and belts. Wampum was woven into designs recording special events, and used for peace gifts as well as trade.

Early British and Dutch settlers used wampum to trade with the Indians. When there wasn't enough to cover all their trading activity, colonists made their own.

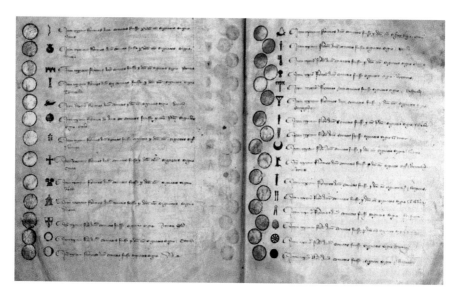

These records of the Officials of the Mint in the city-state of Florence in the 1400s show the details of the designs of the various coins they made to use for money.

Bits and pieces of various metals gained early use as money. In Sumer, an ancient Middle Eastern society that was one of the first known cities, money was based on the weight of a lump of gold or silver. A mina weighed about one pound; 60 shekels equaled one mina. Along with the scarcer gold and silver, pieces of bronze were valued according to their weight. But there was no uniformity of standards, and much confusion and arguing took place.

Unlike shells, stones, and beads, which had no other practical use except to trade for more useful goods, metal could be melted down and made into tools or utensils. Bronze, an alloy of mostly copper and tin, has been used for money since about 3500 B.C. Strong and durable, bronze objects more than 3,000 years old can be found in many museums. Bronze was used for making weapons, statues, tools, cookware, and money.

In ancient Greece, lumps of metal were often measured by the handful. When the Greeks began to make coins, they called one of them tetradrachma—"four hands full" in Greek. Greek money is still called drachma. The Greeks, who controlled vast silver mines, used that money extensively in

The First Bankers

In the 12th and 13th centuries, at the time of the Crusades and Marco Polo's journeys to China, gold was universally accepted as payment among merchants and traders. But gold is heavy, and bandits and pirates preyed on ships and caravans traveling between Europe, the Middle East, and Asia. One day, probably in the 1500s, a goldsmith, someone who makes things from gold, offered to store a merchant's gold for a small fee of part of the gold. In exchange, the goldsmith gave the merchant a deposit receipt called a letter of credit. The merchant could then go about his business without the burden of carrying the gold. He felt safe from thieves, since the receipt had no value unless it was redeemed at the goldsmith's shop. The bank notes were said to be "good as gold."

Gradually the goldsmith realized that nobody ever came for the gold. So he began issuing receipts to people who had no gold, in effect lending them the gold that was stored with him, and charging interest on the loans. There were now more receipts for gold than he could redeem, but nothing would happen unless everybody with a receipt came to collect their gold at the same time. If that happened, he would be in big trouble. These goldsmiths were probably the first bankers.

Commercial banking dates from 1587 in Venice, where the Banco di Rialto did business on a bench by the side of a canal. The word "bank" comes from "banco," the Italian word for bench.

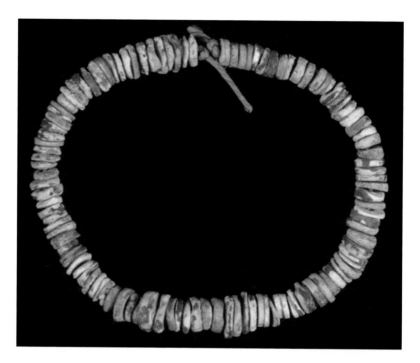

Beads like these, made from clam shells, were strung together and used as money by the Native Americans long before white settlers arrived. Called wampum, the beads were difficult to make, which limited their supply and gave them value.

their coins. Eventually they issued coins of various weights and values, to facilitate making change.

Nobody can be certain where the first standardized coins were invented. It may have been in China or India around 3,000 years ago. The Chinese are known to have replaced bronze tools with tool-shaped tokens around 1100 B.C. About 500 years later, a country called Lydia, in an area that is now part of Turkey, began making oblong coins of gold and silver. The king ordered a design—a lion and bull facing each other—stamped on each coin as an official guarantee that they were all the same weight and value. Different shapes indicated different weights. As a result,

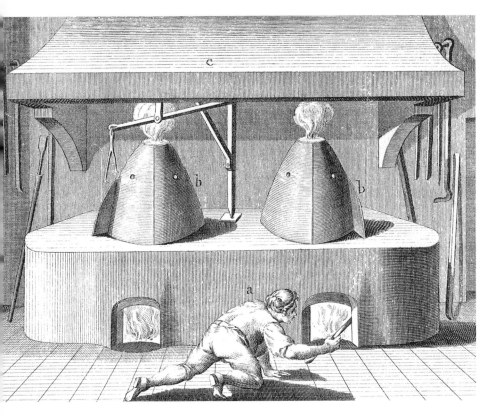

Early French money was based on silver. Silver bars were cast from a furnace like this one, heated by wood. A crucible for melting the bars fit under the hoods.

traders no longer had to carry a set of scales. The coins, called staters, enabled a farmer to exchange a cow or goat for staters, then use the staters to buy something he needed, such as cooking oil and a bronze pot to cook with.

Word of this new system of trading spread quickly. Soon the Greeks began issuing coins made in molds, with pictures of the goddess Athena on one side and an owl on the other. The Romans followed the example set by their Greek predecessors. Kings had their own faces put on the coins. Coins were issued to commemorate victories in battle, a new emperor, or a conqueror such as Alexander the Great.

Owls, turtles, fish, horses, and figures from mythology were popular designs.

One result of emperors and kings setting out to rule the world was the introduction of uniform practices throughout the conquered lands. The standardized coins issued by Alexander the Great, king of Macedonia, and later by the first Roman emperors, became accepted in lands all around the Mediterranean and led to increased trade.

The Macedonians made coins of silver, as well as gold. Silver is very soft; gold is harder and scarcer. Thus the standard rate became 10 silver coins for one gold.

The Value of Gold

People have always been fascinated by gold. Many members of Christopher Columbus's crew died seeking gold in the Caribbean islands where they first landed. When European explorers discovered gold mines in West Africa, they eagerly traded salt, which was necessary for life, for gold, a yellow metal that lasts forever but has little practical use.

All the gold that has ever been mined and refined in the history of the world still exists today. Gold does not rust, erode, or disintegrate. Gold coins found in ancient shipwrecks have been unaffected by the salt water.

Gold in any shape or form is acceptable in trade almost anywhere in the world. People in countries where wars were frequently fought and paper money's value fluctuated widely, often buried gold coins under floorboards or concealed them in walls to use in case they had to escape. Refugees fleeing from one country to another carried gold with them. They knew it would be accepted for food or passage where paper money might not.

Shells like this tiger cowrie are probably the oldest form of money, dating back at least 10,000 years. Found along many coasts of the Pacific and Indian Oceans, cowries were widely used as money in India, Africa, and Asia as recently as the 18th century.

The Chinese invented paper almost 2,000 years ago, and paper money came into use in China in the seventh century A.D. As wealthy traders amassed huge piles of heavy metal coins, they ran out of secure storage room. It was also cumbersome to make large transactions. It took a wagon-load of coins to make an expensive purchase.

To solve these problems, the emperor created a government storage center where the coins could be kept, and he issued pieces of paper representing the amount of coins deposited. The merchant, or anyone else, could turn in the paper and get the coins whenever he wanted them. This enabled the businessman to close a deal by handing the seller a piece of paper instead of lugging the coins around with him. And the seller, if he wished, could redeem the note for the coins, or use it in another transaction.

The Venetian explorer Marco Polo reported that paper money was accepted throughout China because the emperor Kublai Khan decreed that it be so. Any man who refused to accept paper money, Polo wrote, did so "on pain of losing his life."

Since few people bothered to turn in the paper money for coins, the emperor felt free to print and hand out as much of the paper money as he wished. Now there was more paper money in people's hands than there were coins that it could be exchanged for. Instead of trading one piece of paper for a coin, you had to trade two or three pieces of paper if you wanted one of the coins. So merchants raised their prices, demanding more of the paper in exchange for their goods.

When Marco Polo returned to Venice from his travels in China in the 13th century and told stories about the paper money, people shook their heads. They did not understand how a piece of paper could be good for anything. They certainly wouldn't trade their silks or spices or fish for anything as useless as a piece of paper with someone's name on it. Gold, they said, was something with real value. You couldn't sit in a shop and make gold. It had to be found in gold mines and refined. It was scarce.

It would be another 400 years before paper money began to be used in Europe. And ever since then, it has been both a useful invention and a problem.

The Department of the Treasury is responsible for issuing new currency to replace old, worn bills, which are burned. It took a long time for paper money to be trusted in some parts of the globe. Today the American dollar is the most widely accepted currency in the world.

American Money

The nation that became the wealthiest and most productive on earth began life amid financial chaos that lasted more than 100 years.

Young America was basically a bartering society. Colonists traded with British ship captains, using fur pelts, grain, tobacco—whatever they could produce. Settlers who traded with the Indians used wampum. Some English, Dutch, and French coins circulated, but many people refused to take them. Some royal governors had their own coins made in England, but they were useful only in small areas. Most people relied on barter to get the things they needed.

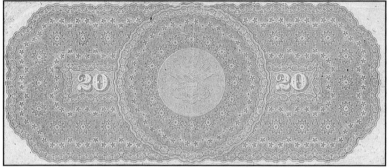

This is a front and back view of a rare 1866 $20 gold certificate. The holder could exchange the bill for $20 worth of gold. Today, paper money can no longer be redeemed for gold or silver.

In 1652 the Massachusetts Bay Colony became the first to get permission from England to make silver coins. But a year later the permit was canceled. The British, trying to force the colonies to trade only with the mother country, prohibited the colonies from making their own coins, which might be used to purchase goods from other countries' ships. The colony secretly continued to make the coins for the next 30 years, shrewdly stamping the year 1652 on all of them.

Massachusetts issued the first colonial paper money in 1690, in the form of receipts for loans of treasure (gold and silver) to pay for the fight against French colonists in New England. Other colonists made their own coins and paper money for local use. This money was often called shillings; America was still part of England, where shillings were the common currency.

During the Revolutionary War the Continental Congress had no money to pay for supplies or soldier's salaries. They did what the emperor Kublai Khan had done in China: print paper money, lots of it. The paper bills were called **Continentals.** They were inexpensive and easy to produce, but nobody trusted the currency. There was no gold or silver behind it. The more the Congress printed, the less it was worth. Soon it became common to describe anything that was useless as "not worth a Continental." Store owners were reluctant to accept it as payment for their precious salt, sugar, tea, and furniture that they had imported all the way from England. They couldn't pay the ships' captains with it. Soldiers used Continentals to wrap their feet at Valley Forge to keep from freezing during the winter. Americans would continue to mistrust paper money for the next 100 years.

When independence was won in 1783, there was real chaos. People who had any money at all owned a mixture of coins and Continentals. Nobody knew what they could spend where, or what it might buy. The barter system still looked more attractive than money. As a result, the salary of one early governor of Tennessee was paid in deerskins.

It took another nine years for the young nation to establish some kind of monetary system, with the dollar as its basis and 100 cents to the dollar. The first national mint in Philadelphia produced $10 gold eagles, silver dollars, and smaller coins. The government set a value on coins based on their weight. Sixteen ounces of silver equaled one ounce of gold. Later, when gold was discovered in the west and it became more plentiful than silver, the ratio was reversed.

But there was no official national paper money. During the next 40 years, Congress authorized two national banks to issue notes that could be exchanged for gold. That ended in 1836. Then things really got confusing. For the next 30 years any bank in the country could print its own banknotes. There were hundreds of them. Notes issued by banks in one state might not be accepted by stores in other states, or by other banks. They were all supposed to be backed by silver or gold coins, but many banks printed more notes than they had coins to back them, just as the Chinese emperor and the goldsmiths of Europe had done. When too many people tried to turn in their banknotes for gold, banks that didn't have enough in reserve closed their doors. Others went broke.

Millions of people were struck with worthless paper currency again. They had confidence only in gold and silver coin money, known as **specie,** not in paper. The situation got so bad, merchants and landowners wouldn't take paper money. The problem was, there wasn't enough gold and silver in circulation to support a growing economy. A man couldn't sell his land or his crop if he insisted on being paid in gold and nobody had any gold to pay him. As a result,

Making Change

The first coins in the western hemisphere, called eight reales, or "pieces of eight," were minted by the Spaniards in Mexico City in 1536. These coins made their way to the early colonies in Virginia and Maryland. Made of soft silver, they were easily cut into eight pieces to make change. A quarter of the coin equaled two pieces or "bits." Today the phrase "two bits" is still used as slang for a quarter of a dollar.

During the Civil War there was a shortage of metal. Coins to make change were scarce. The federal government authorized paper coins, like this one, to be printed. Treasury officials put their own faces on the bills.

land prices collapsed. The collapse in price caused financial **panics.**

When the Civil War broke out in 1862, both the Union and the Confederacy cranked up the printing presses and rolled out paper money to pay the bills. The Union money was black on one side and green on the other. It quickly became known as greenbacks. None of this money was redeemable in gold or silver, so nobody knew what it was worth. Whichever side lost the war would find its money worthless. Confederate money is worth something only to collectors today.

As the war went on, a shortage of coins developed. Nobody could make change. Some stores printed their own paper money to give as change, but of course it couldn't be spent anywhere else. To ease the shortage, the Union allowed people to use postage stamps as money. Later they printed paper money in amounts from 3 cents to 50 cents.

Officials and workers in the Treasury Department put their own faces on the bills.

Gradually this fragmented system was replaced by one in which national banks were allowed to print official paper money, which was good anywhere in the country. The government's promise to redeem it for gold or silver at a fixed rate restored confidence in the paper currency. The government also promised to permit the printing of no more money than they had gold or silver to back it. As the economy grew there were periodic shortages of money, which led to economic slumps and panics. In emergencies the gold standard was abandoned; by 1971 it ceased to

Miners bring in gold dust to the C. A. Cook & Co. banking house in California in 1865. Gold was trusted over paper money by many people until the United States created a central banking system in 1913.

There once was such a thing as a six dollar bill. These were printed in Philadelphia, in 1776, and could be exchanged for gold or silver at any time. If they hadn't been exchangeable, nobody would have accepted them.

exist. Today paper money is no longer redeemable for silver or gold.

In 1913 Congress sought to achieve stability in the money supply by creating the **Federal Reserve System,** a central banking authority that issues our paper currency. The Department of the Treasury is in charge of minting coins at locations in Denver, Philadelphia, and San Francisco.

Making fake money, called counterfeiting, is a federal crime. The Treasury tries to design the bills so that they are difficult to copy and fakes are easy to identify. The Secret Service division of the Treasury Department has the job of tracking down counterfeiters when fake bills show up.

Inflation and Deflation

Inflation is a word used to describe any set of conditions that cause the buying power of money to decline. The word inflation actually conveys an image opposite to its meaning. The value of money itself does not get larger, like a balloon; it shrinks. It's the prices of things that become inflated and rise like a balloon.

Suppose you get an allowance of $5 a week. You spend it on things you want. If the prices of those things go up to $5.50, your allowance will no longer buy as much. it has lost some of its buying power. You either have to get a raise to keep up with the inflated prices, or do without something.

Higher prices may result from an increase in the manufacturer's cost of raw material or the cost of wages paid to employees. Increases in the cost of raw materials or wages can be caused by several things: less competition, enabling the only supplier to raise prices; a country printing too much money with not enough goods for people to spend it on; or unexpected shortages.

When the prices of goods and services go up, workers may demand higher wages to keep up with the rising prices. This forces their employers to raise their prices in order to earn a profit. The higher prices then lead to another

The Danger of Inflation

Sometimes inflation devours the value of money so rapidly, the entire economic system collapses. In the 1920s, following Germany's defeat in World War I, the German government printed so much paper money (called marks), they flooded the country with it. But there was so little food and other goods available to buy, the people didn't care how many millions of marks they spent on a loaf of bread or a bit of sugar. And the baker or store owner kept demanding more of the near-worthless currency in exchange for their precious bread and sugar. Prices soared, not just overnight, but by the minute. Workers demanded to be paid every hour so they could throw the money out the window to their wives, who would try to run to the store before the prices went up again.

It was the classic definition of inflation: too much money chasing too few goods.

If you want to compare prices or incomes from the past to today's money, check out the Inflation Calculator website at www.westegg.com/inflation.

round of higher wages. This process repeats and wages and prices continue to go up; it is called an **inflationary spiral.** Today many labor contracts and pensions like Social Security provide automatic raises based on increases in **cost of living.**

Higher **interest** rates can affect the total cost of things. it becomes more expensive to borrow money to buy a car or house, or to use a **credit card,** even if the price of what you're buying hasn't gone up.

Competition, or lack of it, affects prices. If only one company makes a product or supplies a service, it can raise prices more easily than if there are other companies providing the same goods or services. One gas station in town can charge more than it could if there are six gas stations. One airline flying between two cities may charge higher fares than if there are three or four airlines flying the same route.

Sometimes businesses set out to create a **monopoly**—to control an industry by being the dominant, if not the only, company in the business. John D. Rockefeller tried to create a monopoly in the oil business 100 years ago. He used a variety of methods: cutting his prices below cost and losing money for awhile, until his competitors could not match his prices and had to sell out to him or go out of business; controlling the railroads that moved the oil, and the refineries that processed oil into gasoline.

Federal antitrust (antimonopoly) laws were passed, breaking up Rockefeller's company into smaller ones. The same laws have been used recently against Microsoft for its efforts to dominate some aspects of the computer software business.

For many years telephone and electric companies were granted monopolies to serve certain territories. State governments regulated and limited the prices they could charge

Nowhere did paper money lose its value faster than in Germany in the 1920s. After losing World War I, the German government tried to revive their economy by printing money, lots of money. There was so much of it, and so little to buy with it, merchants kept raising their prices throughout the day.

and profits they could make. But today new technology has resulted in the deregulation of those industries, and there is competition. Lower long distance telephone prices are one result.

Another form of inflation occurs when a government prints more money to keep up with rising prices. Paper and ink for printing money cost very little; governments can print as much as they want. This leads to an inflationary spiral: the more they print the less value it has, and prices go up in a hurry. The cost of things like bread and milk might double in a week, and keep going up. Some South American countries have experienced this kind of inflation.

Suppose you had a Pokémon card that nobody else had. Maybe it was the only one of its kind in the world. How much do you think that someone might give you for it? Some old baseball cards are so rare that people have paid even more than $1 million to own them. This is called the law of supply and demand: when something is rare—maybe the only one in the world, and the demand for it is high—a lot of people want it, its value for those people goes way up. That's what happens with anything in short supply. It could be food or gasoline, a rare stamp, or an autograph of a famous person. Have you ever heard anyone on a hot day say "I'd give anything for a cold drink right now?" What they're saying is that they would pay more for that drink at that moment than they would on a cooler day or if they had a cooler full of soda with them. That's the law of supply and demand at work.

If the oil producing countries of the world cut back on the production of oil, creating a shortage, oil prices will go up, followed by higher prices at the gas station. Bad weather can ruin a crop of oranges or coffee and cause shortages resulting in higher prices for these items. Local wars can cut off the supply of metals or minerals vital to industrial nations.

The federal government keeps track of inflation by monitoring the cost of living—what hundreds of items cost

The Role of the Federal Reserve

The Federal Reserve is the central bank of the United States. Through its 25 branches, it maintains accounts where government income is deposited and checks are written, just like an individual's checking account.

The Federal Reserve supervises the banking industry, enforcing regulations. It also manages the nation's money supply; collects and processes checks; supplies cash to banks when they need additional currency or coins; and wires money and **securities** from one bank to another.

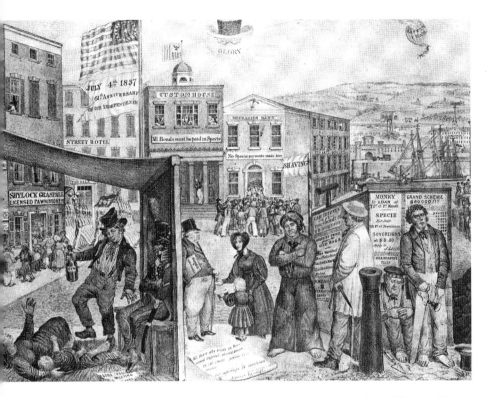

In the early years of the United States people trusted only gold and silver as reliable forms of currency. When these were in short supply, banks closed their doors, and people lost their savings. This 1837 illustration shows the effects of such a panic.

in different parts of the country: food clothing, shelter, entertainment, medical care, electric and heating and telephone bills, taxes, and transportation. A **Consumer Price Index** measures how much the prices of necessary items are changing. If their collective prices increase by, say three percent over a year's time, the official rate of inflation for that year is three percent. About half the wage earners in the country, and all retirees receiving Social Security, get automatic annual raises based on the rate of inflation.

The average rate of inflation in the United States over the past 10 years has been three percent. Unexpected events can result in sharply higher inflation. Wars usually cause temporary shortages of essential materials and food. During the Civil War in 1864, America suffered its highest one-year inflation. Prices rose 27 percent. During World War II, from 1941 to 1945, the government froze prices to prevent a similar experience.

When an oil shortage led to long lines at gas stations and skyrocketing prices in 1979 and 1980, the United States recorded its worse peacetime inflation in history: 13.5 percent.

Inflation does its greatest damage over a long time, eroding the value of savings like termites eating the foundation of a house: slowly, silently, unnoticed, until the damage has been done. Suppose you had put a dollar away in your piggy bank 10 years ago and left it there. Today it would be worth only about 60 cents. It still looks like the same dollar bill you tucked away; the piece of paper didn't shrink. But what it will buy—its buying power—is less than it was.

Deflation is the opposite of inflation; nobody has much money to spend, or there is too much of everything for sale and not enough people want it or can afford to buy it. So prices go down. Sometimes one area of the economy might be affected while other parts are not. Overbuilding of houses or office buildings can result in home prices and rents coming down. Oversupply is the opposite of shortage.

During the Great Depression of the 1930s, when millions of Americans were unemployed and the economy was almost at a standstill, prices declined for four years in a row, from 1929 to 1933. Crop prices plummeted. Farmers were unable to make their mortgage payments and lost their farms. Banks closed, wiping out people's savings and leaving them with no money to buy anything, no matter how cheap it was. Prime real estate on New York's Fifth Avenue was selling for peanuts, but nobody had any peanuts.

Governments worry about both inflation and deflation. They try to maintain the stability of the economy and the value of their money. Some things, like the weather and regional wars, are beyond their control. But there are some things they can manage. How well they do it influences the economic health of the country.

The Federal Reserve Board or "the Fed," as it is sometimes called, supervises the banking system and controls the amount of money in circulation in the United States. If the Fed's governors think there is too much money available for people to borrow and spend, raising the fear of inflation, they can "tighten" the supply of money to slow things down. If business is slow and they want to stimulate spending, the Fed can step up the flow of money into the economy. It works like a faucet: through various means they can open or close the faucet as much as they think advisable.

The Fed can raise and lower interest rates, which affects the cost of borrowing money. Higher interest rates make it more costly for individuals and businesses to borrow money. A family that might qualify for a mortgage on a house, or a loan to buy a new car, at an interest rate of six percent, might not be able to borrow the money if interest rates are eight percent. The higher monthly payments might be more than they can afford.

If the economy is slumping and few people can buy new cars or homes, the Fed might lower interest rates to encourage more spending. If people are borrowing and spending too much money, the Fed might raise interest rates to slow down the amount of buying that people are doing.

None of these systems is perfect. The people in charge of the Federal Reserve System might act too quickly or slowly, or they may misjudge the extent of a business boom or slowdown. It is important to understand that nothing, including the value of your money, is constant, unchanging, or guaranteed.

In 1999 the Federal Reserve Bank of Philadelphia unveiled new versions of $5 and $10 bills. Laid side by side, it's easy to see how the new bills differ from the old ones, with larger, slightly off-center portraits. The new design is harder to counterfeit.

How Banks Work

Do you have a bank in your room at home? It could be in the shape of a football, a cash register, an old car or radio, or an animal. There is usually a slot in it where you put in the money, and a way to open it to take the money out. That kind of bank is a place to save money where you know it's safe so that it will be there when you want it. But putting your money in a piggy bank won't earn you any interest on your savings. For that, you'll have to put your money in a savings bank or other financial institution.

Commercial banks provide a safe place for people to save their money, but banks do much more than that. They make it

For hundreds of years banking was a private business conducted by people like this 16th century couple. They would issue receipts or notes for gold left with them, and lend notes backed by the same gold to people who needed money. This is basically how banks operate today, accepting deposits from people and lending the money out to others.

easier and more convenient for people to pay bills, and when individuals or businesses need money, banks lend it to them.

Here's how it works:

Suppose you have a paper route, or you earn money doing chores, or people give you some money for your birthday. You can take that money to a bank and deposit it in a savings account. The bank will pay you interest (a fee for allowing them to use your money while they hold it for you). Your money is safe and it is earning more money for you. You can take some or all of it out any time you want it.

Some people deposit money in a checking account. This kind of account may or may not pay interest. The main purpose of a checking account is convenience. Most people have bills to pay every month: mortgage payments or rent, car payments, credit card payments, and utility bills. An electric bill may be $47.53. Instead of putting $47 dollars, two quarters, and three pennies in an envelope and mailing

When All the Banks Closed

During the Great Depression of the 1930s, more than 25 percent of working Americans were unemployed. People could not make their payments to the banks holding mortgages on their farms and homes. Businesses also shut down without paying off their bank loans. As a result, many banks ran out of money as people tried to withdraw their savings to buy food. If a bank closed its doors before its depositors could get their money out, the money was lost. When that happened, people panicked, banging on the doors of the banks and demanding their money.

To stop this run on the banks, on March 6, 1933, newly-elected President Franklin D. Roosevelt ordered all banks to close. A week later the government allowed only those banks to reopen that had enough cash to meet the demand. Congress also passed a law insuring people against losing their money even if a bank went out of business in the future. Today, deposits up to $100,000 are insured in member banks of the Federal Deposit Insurance Corporation (FDIC).

it, you can write a **check** for that amount. Rather than carry a lot of cash, some people use checks to pay for things at the supermarket or other stores.

When you write a check for a store, the store deposits it in their own checking account. It is then sent to your bank for collection, and your bank deducts the amount of the check from your account. An average of 25 checks per month are written on every household checking account.

Banks periodically send their customers statements that show the checks that have been written and charged to their account. It's important for anyone who writes checks to keep track of how much money they have left in their account.

Suppose someone has $50 in their account and they write a check to a store for $100. They have **overdrawn** their account; there is not enough money to cover the check. The bank will "bounce" the check back to the store, which may charge a fee for the returned check. If the $100 isn't paid, the person who wrote the bad check may go to jail.

Businesses use banks in the same way as individuals. Retail stores deposit the day's receipts in a bank because it's safer than trying to hide the money somewhere in the store. Businesses also have bills to pay, so a checking account is essential to them.

What do banks do with the money that people deposit with them? The Federal Reserve System, an agency that supervises banks, requires them to hold a certain amount of cash in their vault in reserve, in case a lot of people want to withdraw their money. The rest is used to lend to individuals and businesses. That money enables people to borrow in order to buy things they could never afford if they had to pay for them in full right away, such as cars, houses, home improvements, and college tuition. Businesses borrow to

Throughout American banks were usually the grandest, most imposing building in cities and small towns alike. Many were modeled after Philadelphia's Bank of Pennsylvania, shown here as it looked in 1799. In 1788 there were only three banks in the new United States.

expand, buy new equipment, build factories and office buildings, buy merchandise, or acquire other companies.

If everybody had to save up enough money to pay cash for everything they bought, the entire economy would stop and millions of people would be out of work.

Banks earn a profit by charging interest on the money they lend. It is usually a percentage of the amount you borrow, and it is based in part on your credit rating. Do you pay your bills on time? How much debt do you already have? Do you have enough income to be able to make the payments? It pays to maintain a good credit rating all your life.

Banks usually require **collateral** for a loan, something they can claim if the debt is not paid. A house may be collateral for a mortgage, a type of loan that enables you to buy a house. If the mortgage is not paid, the bank can take the house and sell it to get its money back. If you take out a loan to buy a car, the car itself is the collateral. Other property may be used to back the loan. A person's good reputation may be enough security for the bank.

There are several types of banks: savings banks that make loans primarily for home building and mortgages, and credit unions that provide savings accounts and loans for employees, a company, or members of a particular union or association.

Today financial transactions are increasingly being accomplished by the use of magnetic cards and other electronic means. Many people have their paychecks or Social Security payments deposited directly into their bank accounts. Personal banking business can be done by telephone or computer. Large multinational corporations have their banks transfer billions of dollars to other banks around the world. These electronic transfers move trillions of dollars every day in a few seconds.

The most popular electronic device in use today is the **Automated Teller Machine (ATM).** It enables you to use a card to deposit money or withdraw cash from your account at any time of the day or night, using any ATM in the country.

An ATM card for a bank in New York can be used in an ATM in California. In a split second the bank in New York tells the California machine if you have enough money in your account to cover what you wish to withdraw.

Another card called a **debit card** is growing in popularity. A debit card does the same thing as writing a check on your checking account. Stores prefer it to checks because it requires no ID, reduces handling time and work, and cannot bounce like a bad check. If there's not enough money in the account, the card's use will be rejected by the device at the checkout counter. The money is immediately deducted from the customer's checking account and credited to the store's account. Customers like it because they don't have to write a check or show any ID. Debit cards are also good anywhere in the country.

Credit cards can also be used instead of writing checks. Credit cards, which may be issued by banks, stores, or other businesses, are instant sources of loans. Once you have been approved for a card, you may use it to buy just about anything. You can even use one credit card to pay off the debt on another credit card. Most credit cards require a minimum payment each month, and have limits on how much you can borrow. There is usually no interest charged if the balance you owe is paid off each month. The interest rates charged on credit card debt is much higher than on bank loans.

Some economists predict that America will one day become a cashless society. All transactions will be done with credit and debit cards, toll cards, telephone cards, checks, and electronic transfers of money. That may not happen right away; for now, vending machines and small purchases still require cash. But the trend has been one of less dealing in cash and greater use of technology in the world of money and banking.

ATM—Automated Teller Machine used to deposit or withdraw money

Bank—a business that borrows money from depositors and other banks and lends it to businesses and consumers

Barter—the trading of goods and services without the use of money

Check—a printed form used to pay for something using money in a bank checking account

Collateral—property pledged by a borrower to protect the interests of a lender

Commodities—articles of trade that are useful and valuable

Consumer Price Index—an index measuring the change in the cost of typical goods and services

Continentals—paper bills issued by the Continental Congress of the American colonies

Cost of living—what necessities such as shelter, food, and clothing cost in different parts of the world

Cowrie shell—a type of shell used as currency

Credit card—a plastic card enabling the cardholder to buy something with borrowed money, then pay for it at a later date

Currency—money issued by a national government

Debit card—a plastic card that electronically transfers funds from your bank account when you make purchases

Debt—something that is owed; also the state of owing something to someone else

Deflation—a decline in prices, raising the buying power of money

Federal Reserve System—a government agency that regulates the cost and supply of money and oversees the banking system in the United States

Great Depression—a period during the 1930s when the American economy was in severe decline, leading to widespread poverty and unemployment

Inflation—an increase in prices, reducing the buying power of money

Inflationary spiral—rising prices followed by rising wages which result in more rising prices and more rising wages

Interest—a charge for borrowed money

Money—a medium of exchange used to buy and sell goods and services and to settle debts

Monopoly—a

Mortgage—a loan offered by a bank, usually to help borrowers purchase or build a home

Overdrawn—having written checks for more than the balance available in an account

Panics—when a lot of people are afraid of losing their money, and they all try to sell their stocks or take their money out of the banks at the same time

Securities—another term for stocks and other kinds of investments

Serf—a low-ranking member of a Medieval society who is subservient to a lord and works the land in exchange for a share of food and a place to live

Specie—coin money such as gold or silver

Wampum—beads of polished shells strung in strands and used by North American Indians as money

Federal Reserve Board. *The Federal Reserve System: Purposes and Functions.* Washington, D.C.: Federal Reserve System, 1994.

Grimshaw, Caroline. *Money.* Chicago: World Book Inc., 1998.

Rendon, Marion B. and Rachel Kranz. *Straight Talk About Money.* New York: Facts on File, 1992.

Resnick, Abraham. *Money.* San Diego: Lucent Books, 1995.

Schwalberg, Carol. *From Cattle to Credit Cards; The History of Money.* New York: Meredith Press, 1969.

Valliant, Doris. *Personal Finance.* Philadelphia: Chelsea House Publishers, 2002.

NORMAN L. MACHT is the author of more than 30 books, many of them biographies for Chelsea House Publishers. He is the president of Choptank Syndicate, Inc. and lives in Easton, Maryland.